D1134499

SEX TIPS

FOR HUSBANDS & WIVES FROM 1894

RUTH SMYTHERS

SEX TIPS FOR HUSBANDS AND WIVES 1894

First published in 1894
This edition © Summersdale Publishers 2008

Summersdale Publishers Ltd
46 West Street
Chichester
West Sussex
PO19 1RP
UK

www.summersdale.com

Printed and bound by Tien Wah Press

ISBN: 978-1-84024-702-2

SEX TIPS

FOR HUSBANDS & WIVES FROM 1894

RUTH SMYTHERS

INSTRUCTION AND ADVICE
FOR THE YOUNG BRIDE

on the Conduct and
Procedure of the Intimate
and Personal Relationships
of the Marriage State
for the Greater Spiritual
Sanctity of this Blessed
Sacrament
and the Glory of God

by
Ruth Smythers
beloved wife of
The Reverend L. D. Smythers
Pastor of the Arcadian
Methodist Church of the
Eastern Regional Conference
Published in the year
of our Lord 1894
Spiritual Guidance Press
New York City

To the sensitive young woman who has had the benefits of proper upbringing, the wedding day is, ironically, both the happiest and most terrifying day of her life.

On the positive side, there is the wedding itself, in which the bride is the central attraction in a beautiful and inspiring ceremony...

... symbolising her triumph
in securing a male to provide
for all her needs for the
rest of her life.

On the negative side, there is the wedding night, during which the bride must pay the piper, so to speak, by facing for the first time the terrible experience of sex.

At this point, dear reader,
let me concede one
shocking truth.

Some young women actually
anticipate the wedding night
ordeal with curiosity and
pleasure! Beware such
an attitude!

A selfish and sensual husband
can easily take advantage of
such a bride. One cardinal
rule of marriage should
never be forgotten:

GIVE LITTLE,
GIVE SELDOM,
AND ABOVE ALL,
GIVE GRUDGINGLY.

Otherwise what could have
been a proper marriage could
become an orgy of
sexual lust.

On the other hand, the bride's terror need not be extreme. While sex is at best revolting and at worse rather painful...

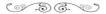

... it has to be endured, and
has been by women since
the beginning of time, and
is compensated for by the
monogamous home and
by the children produced
through it.

It is useless, in most cases, for the bride to prevail upon the groom to forego the sexual initiation.

While the ideal husband would be one who would approach his bride only at her request and only for the purpose of begetting offspring, such nobility and unselfishness cannot be expected from the average man.

Most men, if not denied,
would demand sex almost
every day.

The wise bride will permit
a maximum of two brief
sexual experiences weekly
during the first months
of marriage.

As time goes by she should
make every effort to reduce
this frequency.

Feigned illness, sleepiness,
and headaches are among
the wife's best friends
in this matter.

Arguments, nagging, scolding, and bickering also prove very effective, if used in the late evening about an hour before the husband would normally commence his seduction.

Clever wives are ever on
the alert for new and better
methods of denying and
discouraging the amorous
overtures of the husband.

A good wife should expect to
have reduced sexual contacts
to once a week by the end of
the first year of marriage and
to once a month by the end
of the fifth year of marriage.

By their tenth anniversary
many wives have managed to
complete their child bearing
and have achieved the
ultimate goal of terminating
all sexual contacts with
the husband.

By this time she can depend
upon his love for the
children and social pressures
to hold the husband
in the home.

Just as she should be ever
alert to keep the quantity of
sex as low as possible, the
wise bride will pay equal
attention to limiting the
kind and degree of
sexual contacts.

Most men are by nature
rather perverted, and if given
half a chance, would engage
in quite a variety of the most
revolting practices.

These practices include among others performing the normal act in abnormal positions; mouthing the female body; and offering their own vile bodies to be mouthed in turn.

Nudity, talking about
sex, reading stories about
sex, viewing photographs
and drawings depicting
or suggesting sex are the
obnoxious habits the male is
likely to acquire if permitted.

SAMANTHA
AT SARATOGA

BY
JOSIAH ALLEN'S WIFE

A wise bride will make it
the goal never to allow her
husband to see her unclothed
body, and never allow him
to display his unclothed
body to her.

Sex, when it cannot be
prevented, should be
practised only in
total darkness.

Many women have found it
useful to have thick cotton
nightgowns for themselves
and pajamas for their
husbands. These should be
donned in separate rooms.
They need not be removed
during the sex act. Thus, a
minimum of flesh is exposed.

Once the bride has donned
her gown and turned off
all the lights, she should lie
quietly upon the bed and
await her groom. When he
comes groping into the room
she should make no sound to
guide him in her direction,
lest he take this as a sign
of encouragement.

She should let him grope in
the dark. There is always the
hope that he will stumble
and incur some slight injury
which she can use as an
excuse to deny him
sexual access.

When he finds her, the wife should lie as still as possible. Bodily motion on her part could be interpreted as sexual excitement by the optimistic husband.

If he attempts to kiss her on
the lips she should turn her
head slightly so that the kiss
falls harmlessly on her
cheek instead.

If he attempts to kiss her
hand, she should make a fist.

If he lifts her gown and
attempts to kiss her any place
else she should quickly pull
the gown back in place, spring
from the bed, and announce
that nature calls her
to the toilet.

This will generally dampen
his desire to kiss in the
forbidden territory.

If the husband attempts to
seduce her with lascivious talk,
the wise wife will suddenly
remember some trivial non-
sexual question to ask him.

Once he answers she should
keep the conversation going,
no matter how frivolous it
may seem at the time.

Eventually, the husband
will learn that if he insists
on having sexual contact, he
must get on with it without
amorous embellishment.

The wise wife will allow
him to pull the gown up no
farther than the waist, and
only permit him to open the
front of his pajamas to thus
make connection.

She will be absolutely silent or
babble about her housework
while he is huffing and puffing
away. Above all, she will lie
perfectly still and never under
any circumstances grunt or
groan while the act is
in progress.

As soon as the husband has
completed the act, the wise
wife will start nagging him
about various minor tasks she
wishes him to perform
on the morrow.

Many men obtain a major
portion of their sexual
satisfaction from the peaceful
exhaustion immediately
after the act is over.

Thus the wife must insure
that there is no peace in this
period for him to enjoy.
Otherwise, he might be
encouraged to soon
try for more.

One heartening factor
for which the wife can
be grateful is the fact
that the husband's home,
school, church, and social
environment have been
working together all through
his life to instil in him a deep
sense of guilt in regards to his
sexual feelings...

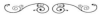

... so that he comes to
the marriage couch
apologetically and filled
with shame, already half
cowed and subdued.

The wise wife seizes
upon this advantage and
relentlessly pursues her
goal first to limit, later to
annihilate completely her
husband's desire for
sexual expression.

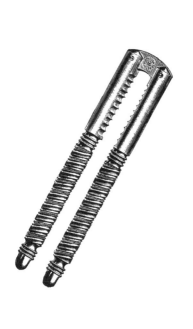

www.summersdale.com